MUSIC for oboe

Oxford

Gordon Jacob

SEVEN BAGATELLES

for solo oboe

Total duration $7\frac{1}{2}$ minutes

To Sarah Francis

SEVEN BAGATELLES

for Solo Oboe

GORDON JACOB

1. March

Alla marcia

mf *f* *p* *cresc.* *f* *p* *f* *p* *cresc.* *f* *f* *p* *cresc* *ff* *p*

© 1971 Oxford University Press

Printed in Great Britain
OXFORD UNIVERSITY PRESS, MUSIC DEPARTMENT, GREAT CLARENDON STREET, OXFORD OX2 6DP

Photocopying this copyright material is ILLEGAL.

2. Elegy

3. Waltz

4. Slow Air

5. Limerick

6. Chinese Tune

7. Galop

Processed and printed by Halstan & Co. Ltd., Amersham, Bucks., England

Oxford Music for Oboe includes:

J. S. Bach *arr. Lawton*	Jesu, Joy of Man's Desiring
Berkeley	Concerto for oboe Fierce Tears I and II Snake Three Moods
Blackford	Posthumus Leonatus
Butler	Chaconne
Crosse	Ariadne
Duck	Impressions
Eichner *arr. Rothwell*	Concerto for oboe and strings
Gardner	Sonata No. 2 for oboe and piano
Haydn *ed. Rothwell*	Concerto for oboe and orchestra
Hoddinott	Bagatelles
Howells *arr. Shannon*	Six Pieces from Lambert's Clavichord
Jacob	Seven Bagatelles Sonatina Ten Little Studies
Lawton	The Young Oboist, Book 1
Ledger	Warlike Music
Maconchy	Three Bagatelles
Mathias	Oboe Concerto
Pergolesi *arr. Barbirolli*	Concerto on Themes of Pergolesi
Powers	In Shadow In Two Minds
Thackray	Nine Short Pieces from Three Centuries
Vaughan Williams	Concerto for oboe and strings (*oboe and piano reduction*)
Vincent *ed. Pratt*	Sonata in C major Op. 1 No. 6
Walton *arr. Palmer*	An Oboe Album

OXFORD UNIVERSITY PRESS

ISBN 978-0-19-357366-6

9 780193 573666